Sewing for
Outdoor Spaces

Sewing for Outdoor Spaces

Easy Fabric Projects for Porch, Patio, Deck, and Garden

Carol Zentgraf

Creative Publishing international

Chanhassen, MN

Copyright © 2006
Creative Publishing international
18705 Lake Drive East
Chanhassen, Minnesota 55317
1-800-328-3895
www.creativepub.com
All rights reserved

Creative Publishing
international

President/CEO: Ken Fund
Vice President/Publisher: Linda Ball
Vice President/Retail Sales: Kevin Haas

Executive Editor: Alison Brown Cerier
Senior Editor: Linda Neubauer
Stylist: Joanne Wawra
Art Director: Brad Springer
Photographer: Andrea Rugg
Production Manager: Laura Hokkanen

Cover Design: Rule 29
Page Design and Layout: Terry Patton Rhoads

Library of Congress Cataloging-in-Publication Data

Zentgraf, Carol.
   Sewing for outdoor spaces : easy fabric projects for porch, patio,
deck, and garden / by Carol Zentgraf.
     p. cm.
     ISBN 1-58923-229-1 (soft cover)
   1. House furnishings. 2. Machine sewing. 3. Outdoor living
spaces--Decoration. I. Title.
     TT387.Z45 2005
     646.2'1--dc22

                2005013656

Printed in China:
10 9 8 7 6 5 4 3 2 1

Portions of this book were previously published in *Outdoor Décor*.

The following companies supplied products for the projects indicated: Beacon Adhesives (Fabri-Tac permanent fabric
adhesive, pages 42, 70, 82, and 88); Fairfield Processing Corp. (NU-Foam upholstery foam alternative, pages 24 and 42
and Soft Touch pillow forms, page 46); Glen Raven, Inc. (Sunbrella fabrics and trims, pages 24, 42, 46, and 82); Prym Dritz
(Wonder Tape double-sided basting tape, pages 54, 70, and 92); Waverly (Sun-N-Shade fabrics, pages 36, 54, and 88).

CONTENTS

Decorating Your Outdoor Spaces   6

Special Fabrics and Materials   8

Outdoor Furniture   12

Custom-Fitted Furniture Cushions   14

Welted Cushions   24

Chair and Bench Pads   30

Garden Chair Slipcover   36

Upholstered Ottoman   42

Decorator Pillows   46

Outdoor Dining   52

Round Tablecloth with Napkins   54

Tablecloths for Umbrella Tables   58

Rectangular Tablecloth with Tied Corners   66

Retro Oilcloth Placemats   70

Outdoor Fun and Relaxation   74

Colorful Hammock   76

Fanciful Hanging Cabana   82

Deluxe Picnic Quilt   88

Nylon Privacy Screen   92

Decorative Flags   96

Windsocks   102

Patterns   108

ABOUT THE AUTHOR

CAROL ZENTGRAF is the author of *Pillows, Cushions, and Tuffets* and *Decorative Storage* and is a regular contributor to several sewing magazines. She lives in Peoria, Illinois.

Acknowledgments

Thanks to Laneventure for supplying the photograph for the front cover. Many thanks to Marge Hols and Mary and Dan Waldrop for allowing us to photograph projects in the wonderful outdoor spaces of their homes.

Decorating Your Outdoor Spaces

One of today's hottest lifestyle trends is to extend the interior of the home to the outdoors. Patios, porches, decks, and gardens are becoming outdoor living spaces decorated for comfort and style. Behind this trend is the introduction of performance fabrics that hold up in outdoor conditions but look like elegant decorator fabrics. *Sewing for Outdoor Spaces* tells how to turn these popular fabrics into custom outdoor décor, making it easy for you to decorate for outdoor living.

Whether you live in a climate where you can enjoy an outdoor space all year long or have a short but treasured summer, you want your outdoor places to be special. And they can be—no matter how much or how little space you have. Even a small balcony can be transformed with a cushioned chair and upholstered ottoman. If you have a large space, consider creating distinct areas for different uses. You might have a dining area, a gathering place for entertaining, and a private retreat with a hammock. Outdoor spaces often seem to need a focal point. Envision a cabana hanging from a tree, with a café table and chair inside. Magical!

Many of the projects can transform the furniture you already have. For example, there are easy, colorful tablecloths to cover your outdoor dining table. You can dress up even the most basic resin chair with a slipcover or make old chairs and lounges more comfortable and stylish by sewing new custom cushions.

Whatever you choose to make, you'll be finished in no time, leaving lots of time to enjoy the new outdoor space you've created!

Special Fabrics and Materials

Sewing for outdoor spaces has become more appealing and more practical because of the many advances in the performance and styling of indoor/outdoor decorator fabrics, trims, and cushions. Before you get started on a project, here's what you need to know about these incredible materials and products.

Indoor/Outdoor Fabrics

Fabric stores now carry water-repellant, fade-resistant fabrics that look and feel like regular decorator fabrics, such as upholstery brocades, printed plain weaves, and textured weaves. These performance fabrics are ideal for exposed areas like decks and patios and for sunrooms and screened porches where sunlight and dampness can damage regular fabrics.

Like other decorator fabrics, many of these special indoor/outdoor fabrics are available in color-coordinated collections that include fabric patterns of different scales, along with stripes, checks, and solids. These collections make it easy to plan coordinating pieces for your outdoor room and to mix and match fabrics for pillows or table linens. Also like indoor deco-

rator fabrics, these new outdoor fabrics are available in light weights to upholstery weights, so you can find the perfect weight for any project from table coverings to durable cushion covers.

For a tablecloth or long cushion, you may need to stitch together lengths of fabrics. For a professional look, you should match the fabric design at the seams. To match prints, buy an extra repeat of fabric. The repeat is the distance from the beginning of a fabric motif to where it begins again along the selvage in the fabric design. Most fabrics have the pattern repeat listed on the identification label, but you can also measure it yourself.

While performance fabrics may look the same as indoor fabrics and are available in some of the same prints and colors, they are dyed, fabricated, and finished differently. The natural fibers, such as cotton, silk, and linen, used for many interior fabrics would weaken and rot when exposed to the elements over time. Many have applied color or designs that fade in direct sunlight, so they aren't recommended for outdoor use. Indoor/outdoor fabrics are made of weather-resistant acrylic or polyester fibers. They have been dyed in the fiber or yarn stage to make them colorfast and are treated to resist stains and mildew.

Sew these indoor/outdoor fabrics as you would any medium-weight decorator fabric, using a size 80 needle and all-purpose polyester sewing thread. If the fabric ravels easily, it's a good idea to finish the edges and seam allowances with zigzag stitching or serging.

Other fabrics, such as canvas and nylon, also are weather resistant and ideal for a number of outdoor projects. Plain canvas provides strong, invisible support for a hammock, for example. Striped canvas works great for a fanciful cabana top. Nylon is ideal for outdoor projects, such as flags and privacy screens. Because nylon is made with dyed filaments that are extruded to make fibers, it is naturally strong, durable, and weather resistant. It blocks wind, is colorfast, and dries quickly. The higher the denier count, the heavier the nylon. When sewing these fabrics, use a size 70 or 80 needle and avoid pinning or ripping seams where the holes will show.

Vinyl oilcloth is a waterproof fabric that is fade, stain, and soil resistant. It is available in a fun array of colors and prints and is practical and attractive for outdoor table coverings and accessories. As with nylon and canvas, holes from pins and needles will show in vinyl oilcoth, so pin only within seam allowances and avoid ripping seams. Use a size 80 needle to sew vinyl oilcloth.

Always ask about care requirements when purchasing these indoor/outdoor fabrics. Some are more weatherproof than others. All can be spot cleaned using mild soap and water, but not all can be machine washed or bleached. For extra protection against the elements, consider using UV protective sprays and water-repellant sprays.

Trims

The companies that produce indoor/outdoor fabrics also offer weather-resistant trims. These trims look the same as other decorator trims but are made of weather-resistant polyester fibers instead of the usual cotton or rayon. Options include twisted welting, brush fringe, and tassel fringe. Trims are available for two types of applications—sew-in or sew-on. Sew-in trims have a lip or extension designed to be sewn into a seam and not seen on the finished project. Sew-on trims have a finished or decorative header designed to show after application. The trims can be sewn on, glued on with fabric glue, or attached with paper-backed fusible adhesive.

Filler Materials

It is important to fill outdoor furniture cushions with drainable outdoor foam. Poly-fil® NU-Foam®, for example, is a compressed polyester upholstery foam alternative that does not hold water or disintegrate and is mildew resistant. It is available in thicknesses ranging from ½" to 4" (1.3 to 10 cm) and is sold by the yard and in precut squares. Foam alternative is easily cut to any shape with sewing shears or a rotary cutter and mat. When cutting thick pieces of NU-Foam, cut in thin layers rather than trying to make a single cut.

Polyester upholstery batting can be used alone to stuff furniture cushions. It can also be wrapped around foam or foam alternative cushions for a thicker look and to soften the edges. This synthetic batting is resilient and naturally weather resistant.

Pillow forms come in several shapes and sizes. Look for square, rectangular, and round forms with a knife edge. Bolster pillow forms in several lengths and diameters and square box-edge forms in several sizes are also available. Select polyester fiber-filled pillow forms; cover them with a plastic bag before inserting in the pillow cover if they will be exposed to rain. You can also look for inexpensive pillow forms with synthetic nonwoven covers that resist weather better than woven cotton covers.

Notions

To complete your outdoor sewing projects, you may also need hook-and-loop tape or zippers for cushions or pillows. Choose a regular or invisible polyester zipper rather than one with metal teeth for best weather resistance.

For wraps, straps, and ties, you will need notions such as nylon strapping or braid. When selecting ribbon for outdoor use, choose polyester or other synthetic fibers.

Sew your projects with all-purpose polyester thread. Nylon monofilament thread is also ideal for projects where you don't want to see the thread.

OUTDOOR FURNITURE

Custom-Fitted Furniture Cushions

ustom-fitted cushions will make your chairs and chaise lounges comfortable and stylish. These soft cushions are filled with layers of polyester upholstery batting and covered with the indoor/outdoor fabric of your choice.

The cushions are sewn with a simple mock-box construction that requires only front and back pieces (no separate sides). Stitching lines across the cushions allow them to bend and conform to the shape of the furniture. Stitching lines can also be used to create a head or leg rest.

MATERIALS

- Paper and pencil

- Indoor/outdoor decorator fabric

- Chalk for marking fabric

- Polyester upholstery batting

- Aerosol adhesive for polyurethane foam

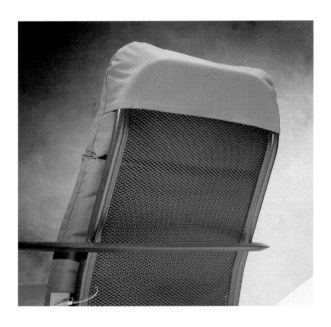

Attachment Styles

Depending on the style of furniture, cushions can be secured with ties or a hood. Plan ahead before you start the project.

Ties can be secured around the frame of many metal and wooden furniture pieces and are sometimes inserted through the openwork of a mesh deck or between straps, bars, or slats. For a cushion that is reversible, stitch the ties at the side seams.

If the furniture does not have any open areas for ties, create a hood to fit over the back. How-to steps for a hood or ties follow later in the project.

Cushions with Rounded Corners

1 Measure the width of the chair or chaise frame from side to side (a). Measure the distance from the top of the frame to the desired depth of the headrest (b). Measure the length of the chair or chaise lounge frame from the top of the back to the front of the frame (c). Measure the distance from the front edge to the back of the seat (d); if the chaise lounge has a curved or bent leg-rest area, also measure the depth of the leg rest from the front edge to the highest point on the frame (e). Record the measurements.

2 Add 4" (10 cm) to the length and width to allow for seam allowances and the thickness of the cushion. In addition, add 2" (5 cm) to the length for each stitching line across the cushion. Cut two pieces of fabric to this size.

3 Trace the upper and lower curved corners of the frame on paper. Trim the paper along the curved lines.

4 Place the pattern for the curves at the corners of the layered fabric, with the marked lines tapering to the raw edges at the top and sides; pin in place. Trim the fabric along the curves.

(continued)

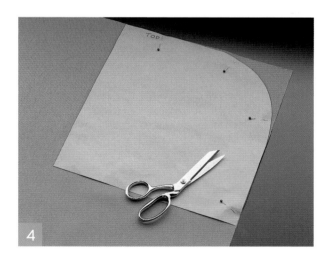

5 Measure from the upper edge of the fabric a distance equal to the desired depth of the headrest plus 3" (7.5 cm). Using chalk, mark a line on the right side of each piece across the width. Mark the ends of the lines on the wrong sides.

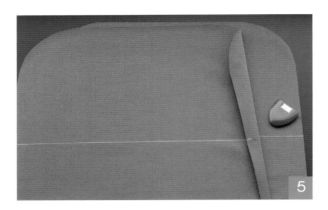

6 *For a chair or chaise lounge with a leg extension (photo below),* measure from the lower edge of the fabric a distance equal to the measurement from the front of the frame to the back of the seat plus 3" (7.5 cm). Using chalk, mark a line across the right side of each piece. Mark the ends of the lines on the wrong sides of the fabric pieces.

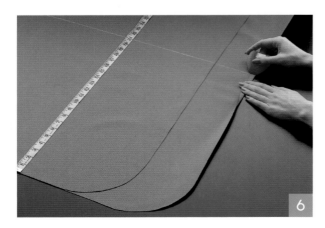

6 *For a chaise lounge with a curved or bent leg rest (photo below),* measure from the lower edge of the fabric a distance equal to the depth of the leg rest plus 3" (7.5 cm); mark a chalk line on the right side of each piece across the width. Also measure from the lower edge of the fabric a distance equal to the measurement from the front of the frame to the back of the seat plus 5" (12.7 cm); mark a chalk line on the right side of each fabric piece. Mark the ends of both lines on the wrong sides of the fabric pieces.

7 Cut and attach the hood piece, if desired (page 22). Place the front and back cushion pieces right sides together; pin, matching the marks on the sides.

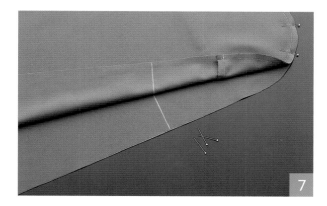

8 Machine-stitch ½" (1.3 cm) from the raw edges, starting on one long side, just beyond the rounded corner; stitch across the end, down the opposite long side, across the opposite end, and stop just beyond the last corner.

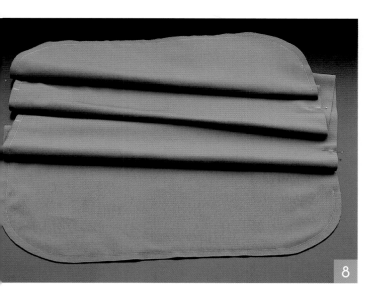

9 Stitch ½" (1.3 cm) from the raw edges on the remaining long side, starting and stopping 2" (5 cm) from each marked line; this leaves an opening in each section of the cushion. Clip the seam allowances of the rounded corners.

10 Turn the cover right side out through one opening. Make and position the ties, if desired (page 23). On the sides of the cushion, fold 1" (2.5 cm) inverted tucks at the stitching lines as shown and pin in place; enclose the ties, if any, in the tucks. Pin the front and back cushion pieces together along the stitching lines.

(continued)

11 Stitch along the marked stitching lines, stitching the tucks in place at the sides. If the cushion has ties, catch the ties in the stitching of the tucks.

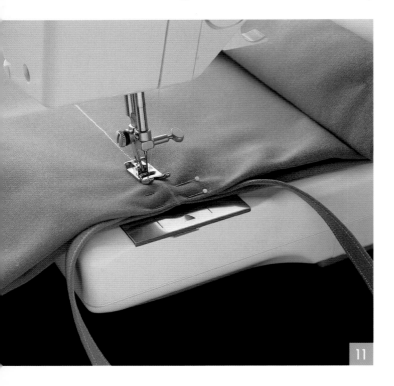

13 Repeat step 12 for the section at the bottom of the cushion, using four pieces of batting 1" (2.5 cm) wider than the frame and 1" (2.5 cm) longer than the measurement from the front of the frame to the back of the seat. If you're making a cushion for a chaise lounge with a leg rest, use pieces 1" (2.5 cm) longer than the depth of the leg rest.

12 Cut four pieces of polyester upholstery batting for the area at the top of the cushion, cutting the pieces 1" (2.5 cm) wider than the chair or chaise lounge frame and 1" (2.5 cm) longer than the depth of the headrest; round the corners. Stack and secure two pieces of batting together, applying aerosol adhesive to both inner sides. Repeat to secure all four layers.

14 Repeat step 12 for the middle section or sections of the cushion, using pieces of batting 1" (2.5 cm) wider than the frame, with the length of each piece equal to the distance between the stitching lines minus 1" (2.5 cm).

15 Fold the layered batting for the head-rest in half crosswise; insert it into the headrest area through the opening, pulling the batting all the way to the opposite side of the cushion. Unfold the batting and smooth it in place. Adjust the position of the batting as needed, filling the corners with pieces of batting, if necessary.

17 Pin the openings on the side of the cushion closed; slipstitch.

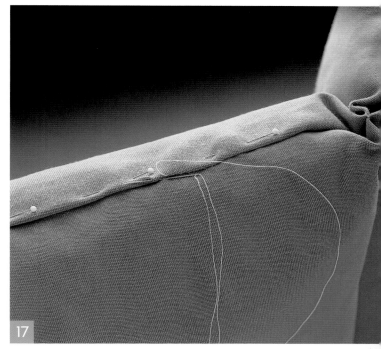

16 Repeat step 15 for the remaining areas of the cushion, using corresponding sections of the batting.

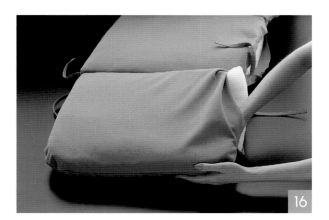

Cushions with Square Corners

1 Measure the chair or chaise lounge frame and cut the fabric as on page 17, steps 1 and 2. At the corners, use chalk to mark a 1½" (3.8 cm) square; cut on the marked lines.

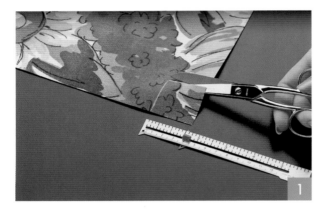

2 Fold the corners, matching the raw edges; stitch a ½" (1.3 cm) seam, 2" (5 cm) long, as shown. Complete the cushion as on pages 18 to 21, steps 5 to 17; in step 7, fold the corner seam allowances of the front and back pieces in opposite directions to distribute the bulk.

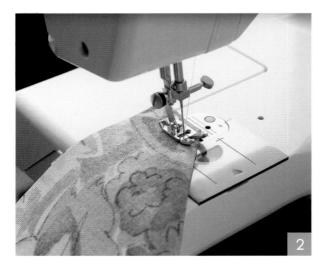

Hooded Back

1 Cut the fabric for the hood piece, 4" (10 cm) wider than the width of the chair or chaise lounge frame and 8½" (21.8 cm) long. For a cushion with rounded corners, trim the upper corners of the hood, using the paper pattern for the upper corners from step 3 on page 17 for Cushions with Rounded Corners.

2 On the lower edge of the hood piece, press under ½" (1.3 cm) twice to the wrong side; stitch to make a double-fold hem.

3 Pin the hood piece to the cushion back piece, right sides up; machine-baste a scant ½" (1.3 cm) from the raw edges. Complete the cushion as on pages 19 to 21, steps 7 to 17.

Ties

1 Cut four 2" x 24" (5 x 61 cm) strips of fabric for the ties. Press them in half lengthwise, wrong sides together; unfold. Fold the raw edges to the center; press.

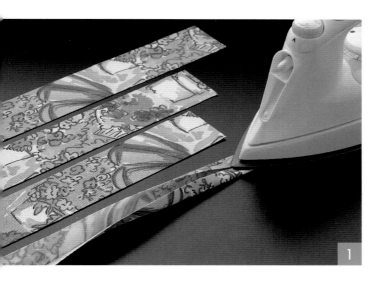

2 Refold the ties in half, enclosing the raw edges. Edgestitch close to both long edges of the ties.

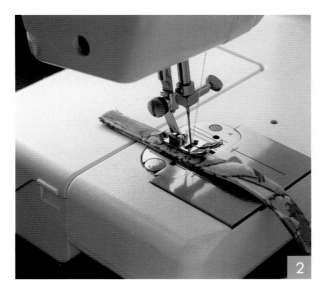

3 Position and pin the ties to the sides of the cushion at the marked stitching lines for the headrest and back of the seat. Complete the cushion as in steps 10 to 17 for Cushions with Rounded Corners.

Welted Cushions

You can renew your outdoor seating by sewing new deluxe cushions. The trend in outdoor chairs and benches is thick, really comfortable cushions. Often two different cushion styles are used on a piece of furniture, such as the firm, boxed seat cushion and softer, mock-box back cushion on this chair.

The same fabric was used for both cushions and all the welting on the chair shown here. However, you may want to mix and match coordinating fabrics, so yardage estimates are given separately for each cushion in the materials list. The amounts listed will make a 20" x 23" (51 x 58.5 cm) seat cushion and a 20" x 20" (51 x 51 cm) back cushion; adjust the yardage as necessary for your cushions.

Welting gives the seams more strength and better definition. Make the welting with polyester filler cord, which is more weather resistant than cotton filler cord. Choose a size that best suits your project and the look you want. Zippers at the back of the seat cushion and at the bottom of the back cushion make it easy to place and remove the inserts.

MATERIALS

- 1 yd. (0.92 m) indoor/outdoor decorator fabric, 54" (137 cm) wide for seat cushion cover

- ⅔ yd. (0.63 m) indoor/outdoor decorator fabric, 54" (137 cm) wide for back cushion cover

- ½ yd. (0.5 m) indoor/outdoor decorator fabric, 54" (137 cm) wide for seat cushion welting

- ½ yd. (0.5 m) indoor/outdoor decorator fabric, 54" (137 cm) wide for back cushion welting

- Nu-Foam upholstery foam alternative, 4" (10 cm) thick

- Medium-tip permanent marker

- Clear quilter's ruler or yardstick

- Polyester filler cord in desired diameter in amount equal to twice the circumference of seat cushion plus circumference of back cushion top and sides

- Seam sealant

- Two polyester zippers in closest length to cushion back width

- Basting tape

- Polyester upholstery batting

- Heavy-duty thread and hand-sewing needle

Cutting Directions

If you are replacing existing cushions that fit the furniture accurately, trace the cushions to make patterns. Otherwise, measure the seat dimensions for the box seat cushion. Draw the pattern on paper and add ½" (1.3 cm) to the outer edge for a seam allowance. Use the pattern to cut two fabric panels for the seat cushion cover. Center any large design motifs or stripe patterns on the panels, positioning the patterns to match the stripes at the seamlines.

For a seat cushion zipper strip with a finished width of 4" (10 cm), cut the strip 6¼" (15.7 cm) wide and 1" (2.5 cm) longer than the zipper length (measured from the top stop to the bottom stop); cut the strip in half lengthwise. Cut the seat cushion boxing strip 5" (12.7 cm) wide to fit the cushion circumference minus the zipper length plus 1" (2.5 cm) for seam allowances; piece as necessary. If working with striped fabric, plan the stripes of the boxing strip to align to the stripes of the cushion cover along the front.

Measure the back dimensions (with seat cushion in place) and trace the shape of the upper back. Draw the pattern on paper. This line will be the cutting line for the cushion insert. Draw the cutting line for the fabric 2 ½" (6.5 cm) from the cushion insert cutting line. Use the pattern to cut two fabric panels for the back cushion cover, centering any large design motifs or matching stripes.

Measure around the filler cord and add 1" (2.5 cm) to determine the width to cut the bias strips. To determine the length of welting strips needed for the seat cushion, measure the cushion circumference and add 6" (15 cm) for the overlap. For box cushions with two welted edges, multiply this measurement by two. To determine the length of welting strips needed for the back cushion, measure the top and sides of the cushion cover.

Making Welting

1 Cut the bias strips and seam them together as in steps 1 and 2 on page 34.

2 Wrap the bias strip around the cording with wrong sides together. Using a zipper or welting foot, machine-baste the layers together close to the cord.

3 Pin or use basting tape to apply the welting to the right side of the cushion cover panel, aligning the raw edges. Begin at the center of the least conspicuous edge. Clip the welting seam allowances up to the stitching at each corner to allow the welting to smoothly turn the corner. If your fabric frays easily, apply a drop of seam sealant to the end of the clip.

4 Begin stitching 1" (2.5 cm) from the welting end. Stitch just inside the basting line. Pivot at the corners. Stop stitching 2" (5 cm) from the point where the ends meet. Leave the needle down in the fabric.

5 Remove several basting stitches from the finishing end and open the fabric to expose the cording. Cut the cording even with the beginning end. Cut the excess fabric 2" (5 cm) beyond the beginning end. Fold under ½" (1.3 cm) of the overlapping bias strip. Lap it around the other end and finish stitching.

5

Box Seat Cushion

1 Trim the ½" (1.3 cm) seam allowance from the pattern. Place the pattern on the NU-Foam and trace the edges with a permanent marker. Repeat on the opposite side of the cushion, making sure the pattern position is identical on each side. Cut the foam alternative along the lines, using sharp shears and cutting in layers.

2 Wrap polyester upholstery batting over the cushion, and trim the edges so they just meet. Trim the batting corners diagonally, and fold them together so the edges just meet. Whipstitch the edges of the batting together, enclosing the cushion.

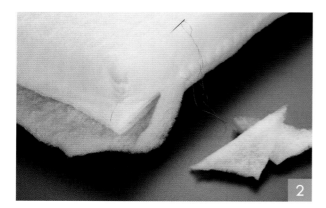

3 Follow the welting instructions (page 27) to make and apply welting to the edges of the top and bottom panels.

4 Pin the zipper strips right sides together. Stitch ⅝" (1.5 cm) seams ½" (1.3 cm) long at the ends. Baste the seam between the stitched ends. Press the seam open.

5 Apply basting tape to the right side of the zipper tapes along the outer edges. Remove the paper backing and center the zipper facedown over the basted part of the seam. Press with your fingers to firmly adhere the tapes to the seam allowances.

6 Using a zipper foot, stitch a continuous rectangle around the zipper ¼" (6 mm) from the teeth and across the ends just beyond the zipper stops.

7 Stitch the ends of the boxing strip to the ends of the zipper strip, right sides together, forming a ring. Press the seams away from the zipper. Remove the basting stitches from the zipper seam.

8 Pin the boxing strip to one panel of the cushion cover, right sides together, with the zipper at the back. Match any stripes at the cushion front. Clip the boxing strip at the corners to allow the seam allowance to open and turn the corner. Use a welting or zipper foot to stitch the layers together along the welting stitching line.

9 Open the zipper partway. Stitch the remaining panel to the other side of the boxing strip as in step 8.

10 Turn the cushion cover right side out through the zipper opening. Press the edges. Insert the cushion into the cover and zip it closed.

Mock-Box Back Cushion

1 Trim the pattern along the cushion insert cutting line. Cut the cushion and wrap it with batting as in steps 1 and 2, opposite. Make and apply welting to the side and top edges only of one cushion cover panel.

2 Fold one of the square bottom corners in half diagonally, right sides together and pin. Measure 2½" (6.5 cm) from the point along the fold and mark a line across the corner perpendicular to the fold. Stitch on the line. Trim the excess

fabric. Repeat for the other corner and for the corners of the other panel. Press the seams open.

3 Pin the lower edges of the panels right sides together, aligning the corner seams. Center the zipper on the bottom edge and mark the seam allowances just beyond the zipper stops. Stitch from 1" (2.5 cm) before the corner seam to the mark at each side of the cushion bottom. Baste the seam between the stitched ends. Press the seam open. Use basting tape to apply the zipper to the basted seam allowances and stitch in place as in steps 5 and 6, opposite. Remove the basting thread.

4 Open the zipper partway. Pin the side and top edges of the panels together. With the welted panel facing up, stitch the panels together just inside the welting basting line, using a welting or zipper foot.

5 Complete the cushion as in step 10, above.

Chair and Bench Pads

Pads add color and style to basic wooden or resin chairs and benches. These lightly padded, reversible seat cushions are simple to sew and feature bias binding around the edges. The bias binding conforms easily to curved edges and rounded corners. Make your own bias binding for a customized look, using a bias tape maker. To speed up the project, you can use purchased bias binding.

Polyurethane foam is used for the inserts in these pads, so they should not be left out in the rain. For more weather resistance, substitute NU-Foam.

MATERIALS

- Decorator fabric

- ½" (1.3 cm) high-density firm polyurethane foam or Nu-Foam upholstery foam alternative

- ½" (1.3 cm) single-fold bias tape; or fabric and ¾" (2 cm) bias tape maker

- Marking pen

- Glue stick

Chair or Bench Pad

1 Make a paper pattern of the chair or bench seat, rounding any sharp corners. Cut the pattern; check the fit. This pattern is used for cutting the fabric.

2 Trace another pattern on a separate piece of paper; mark the cutting line ⅝" (1.5 cm) in from the traced line. Cut out the pattern on the inner marked line. This pattern is used for cutting the foam.

3 Cut the pad front and pad back from decorator fabric, using the pattern for fabric. Place the pattern for foam on the polyurethane foam; trace, using a marking pen. Cut the foam on the marked line, using a rotary cutter and mat or scissors.

4 Make bias tape (page 34) slightly longer than the pad circumference, or use purchased bias tape. Press the bias tape into a curved shape to match the shape of the pad. To prevent puckering, stretch the tape slightly as you press.

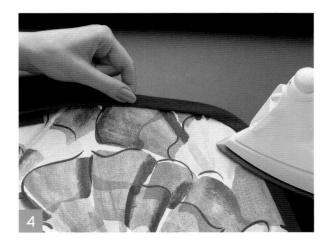

5 Center the foam on the wrong side of the pad back; place the pad front over the foam, right side up, matching the raw edges of the fabric. Pin the layers together.

6 Machine-baste a ¼" (6 mm) seam around the pad, using a zipper foot.

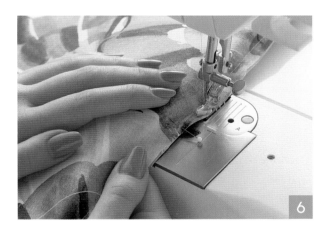

7 Apply a small amount of glue stick to the seam allowance of the pad back. Finger-press the wide side of the bias tape into position, with the raw edges of the pad fabric at the foldline of the tape; overlap the ends of the tape about 1" (2.5 cm).

8 Turn the pad over. Glue-baste the narrow side of the tape to the seam allowance of the pad front, using a small amount of glue stick. Join the ends of the tape by folding under ¼" (6 mm) on the overlapped end; glue-baste.

9 Stitch along the inner edge of the tape, using a zipper foot, with the narrow edge of the tape facing up.

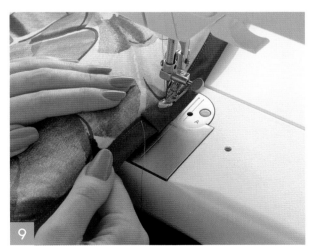

Making Bias Tape

1 Fold the fabric in half diagonally on the bias grain; cut along the fold. Cut bias strips 1¾" (4.5 cm) wide.

2 Join the strips, right sides together, by placing them at right angles, offset ¼" (6 mm); the strips will form a "V." Stitch a ¼" (6 mm) seam across the ends. Press the seam open; trim off the seam allowance points even with the edges. The raw edges match on the long edges after the seam is stitched.

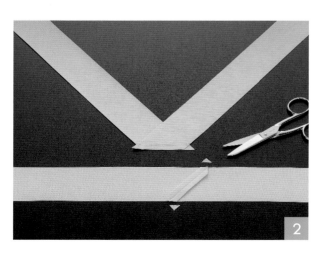

3 Thread the pointed end of the bias strip through the channel at the wide end of the tape maker, bringing the point out at the narrow end. Using a pin, pull the fabric through the slot opening; pin the point of the strip to a pressing surface.

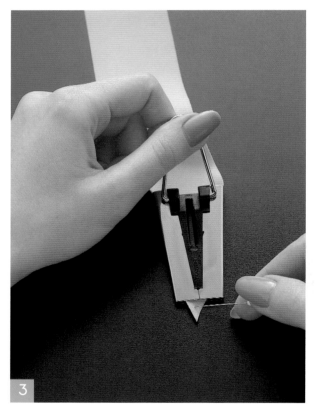

4 Press the folded bias strip as you pull the tape maker the length of the strip. The tape maker automatically folds the raw edges to the center of the strip.

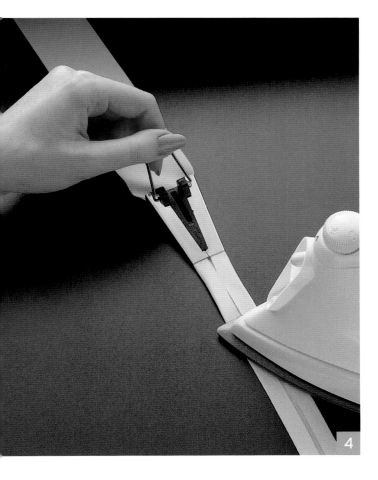

5 Fold the bias tape lengthwise, with the folded edge on the bottom extending a scant ⅛" (3 mm) beyond the folded edge of the upper layer; press.

Garden Chair Slipcover

You can transform a stacking resin chair with a loose-fitting slipcover made of indoor/outdoor decorator fabric. These inexpensive garden chairs come in a variety of shapes and sizes. No one will guess what's under the cover!

To ensure the slipcover fits well, the pattern is created by pin-fitting pieces of inexpensive fabric, such as muslin or sheeting.

This slipcover consists of four pieces: one piece that wraps around the outside, covering the back and arms; one piece that wraps around the inside, covering the back and arms; one seat piece; and a gathered skirt. The inner and outer back pieces are placed with the lengthwise grain running horizontally. They can usually be cut from one width of 54" (137 cm) fabric.

MATERIALS

- Masking tape

- 3½ yd. (3.2 m) muslin, 45" (115 cm) wide

- Medium-tip permanent marker

- Double-stick tape

- Yardstick

- 4½ yd. (4.15 m) indoor/ outdoor decorator fabric, 54" (137 cm) wide

- Water-soluble fabric marker

- 1⅓ yd. (1.23 m) twill tape or grosgrain ribbon

Garden Chair Slipcover

1 Mark the center of the chair at the top of the back and at the front and back of the seat with tape. Measure the chair from the front of one arm, around the back to the front of the other arm (a). Then measure from the top of the back to a few inches below the seat (b). Add 6" (15 cm) in both directions and cut a piece of muslin to this size. Using a permanent marker, mark a vertical line at the center back and mark the lengthwise grainline of the pattern piece.

2 Measure the inside of the chair from the front of one arm, across the back, to the front of the other arm (c). Then measure from the top of the back to the top of the seat (d). Add 6" (15 cm) in both directions and cut a piece of muslin to this size. Mark a vertical line at the center back. Mark the lengthwise grainline of the pattern piece.

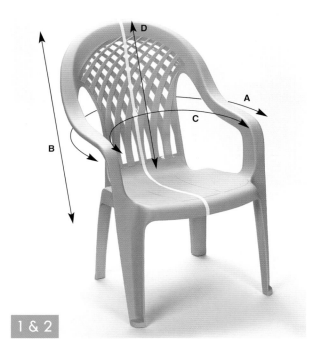

1 & 2

3 Pin the inner and outer patterns together at the center back line. Drape the pinned pattern over the chair, matching the center back lines to the center of the chair. Smooth the inner pattern down over the inner back of the chair, keeping the marked line in the center of the chair. Using double-stick tape, secure the inner pattern to the chair seat at the base of the center line and at the back corners of the seat.

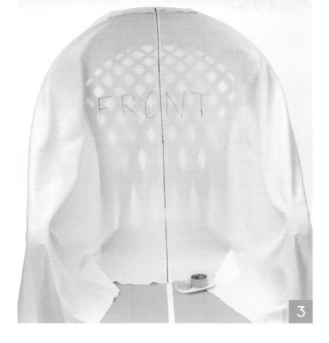

5 Pin excess fullness of the inner pattern into two pleats at the back corners of the seat so the pattern fits as smoothly as possible.

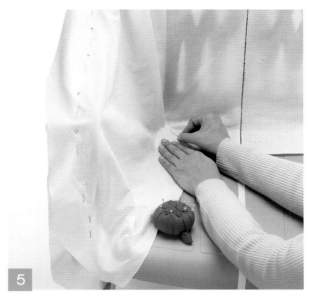

4 Drape the outer pattern around the curve of the chair to the front of the arms, keeping the side grainlines perpendicular to the floor. Pin the inner and outer patterns together along the edge of the chair back and arms. Trim away some of the excess fabric over the arms to make this step easier. At the front of the arms, pin the patterns together in a straight line to the outer front corner of the seat, rather than fitting it to the shape of the arms. Keep the grainlines perpendicular to the floor.

6 Mark the lower edge of the inner pattern along the outer edge of the seat. Mark a point at each front top corner where the upper and inner covers meet. Trim the pattern to 1" (2.5 cm) beyond the marked line. *(continued)*

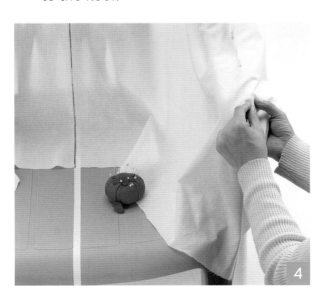

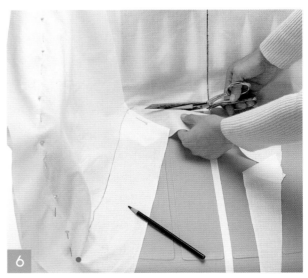

7 Measure the distance from the floor to the lower edge of the seat front. Using a yardstick, mark a line on the outer pattern the same distance from the floor. Trim the pattern to 1" (2.5 cm) beyond the marked line.

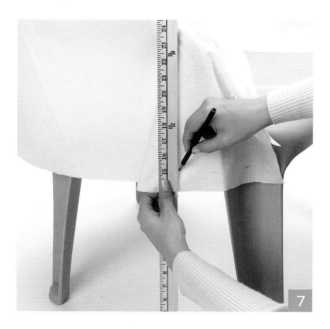

8 Cut a piece of muslin a few inches larger than the chair seat, extending down past the lower edge of the seat front. Mark a center line. Secure the pattern to the chair seat with double-stick tape, aligning the centers. Pin the seat piece to the inner back pattern where it aligns to the marked line on the inner pattern. Mark the front of the seat even with the lower edge of the chair front and the line marked on the lower edge of the outer pattern. Mark the points on the front corners that align to the points where the inner and upper back pieces meet (marked in step 6). Mark the position

of the box pleats at the back corners. Trim the seat pattern to 1" (2.5 cm) beyond the marked line.

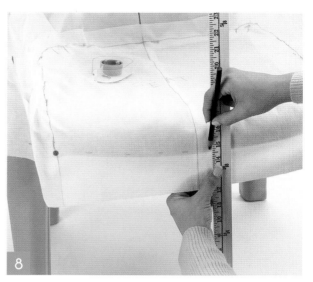

9 Adjust the fit. Mark all the pinned seamlines and the pleats. Mark points where seams intersect and any other points that will be helpful when stitching the slipcover together.

10 Remove the pattern from the chair. Remove the pins. Cut the pattern pieces ½" (1.3 cm) beyond marked seamlines. Fold each piece in half to check for symmetry and adjust the seamlines if necessary. Use the pattern pieces to cut out the decorator fabric. Transfer all marks. For the slipcover skirt, measure from the lower edge of the seat front (same measurement taken in step 7) and add 2½" (6.5 cm) for seam and hem allowances. Cut two strips equal to this measurement across the width of the decorator fabric and trim the selvages.

11 Staystitch the lower edge of the inner back piece a scant ½" (1.3 cm) from the edge. Fold the pleats at the marks and baste in place. Pin the upper edges of the inner and outer back pieces, right sides together, matching marks. Stitch a ½" (1.3 cm) seam.

12 Pin the seat to the lower edge of the inner back, right sides together, aligning the pleats to the marks at the back corners. Clip the seam allowance of the inner back as necessary to allow it to fit around the curves of the seat. The lower front edge of the seat will align to the lower edge of the outer slipcover. Stitch.

13 Sew the short ends of the skirt strips right sides together and press the seams open. Finish one long edge with serging or zigzag stitches. Press under 1½" (3.8 cm) and topstitch the hem in place.

14 Pin-mark the raw edge of the skirt in fourths. Between each set of pin marks, stitch two rows of gathering threads. Also pin-mark the lower edge of the slipcover in fourths.

15 Pin the skirt to the slipcover, right sides together, matching pin marks. Pull each set of gathering threads to evenly gather the skirt to fit the cover; knot the thread ends to secure. Stitch the skirt in place and press.

16 Cut two 24" (61 cm) lengths of twill tape or ribbon. Fold the strips in half and stitch one securely to the seam allowances on the underside of the slipcover at each seat back corner.

17 Put the slipcover on the chair. Lift the skirt and tie the twill tape ties to the back chair legs to hold the slipcover in place.

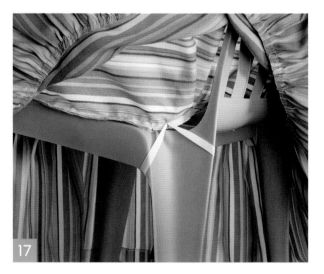

Upholstered Ottoman

This easy ottoman adds a touch of luxury to a porch. It's practical, too—put your feet up or use it for extra seating when you have guests.

The upholstery-weight indoor/outdoor decorator fabric and decorative trims used for this ottoman are weather resistant, though you should not leave the ottoman out in the rain. Purchased wooden legs are secured with metal leg plates to an upholstered wooden circle; all are available at home improvement stores. The legs can be painted with exterior paint or sealed with exterior varnish to make them more durable.

- 21" (53.5 cm) circle of plywood, ¾" (2 cm) thick

- Medium-tip permanent marker

- Yardstick

- Four straight leg plates and 16 screws

- Drill and drill bits

- 21" (53.5 cm) circle NU-Foam upholstery foam alternative, 4" (10 cm) thick

- Permanent fabric adhesive

- 1 yd. (0.92 m) indoor/outdoor decorator fabric, 54" (137 cm) wide for ottoman top

- Heavy-duty staple gun and staples

- Four screw-in furniture legs, 14" (35.5 cm) long

- 1 yd. (0.92 m) indoor/outdoor decorator fabric, 54" (137 cm) wide for ottoman skirt

- Disappearing fabric marker

- 2 yd. (1.85 m) indoor/outdoor tassel fringe with decorative header

Cutting Directions

Place the wood circle on the wrong side of the fabric for the top. Use the fabric marker to draw a line 6" (15 cm) beyond the wood circle. Cut the top out along the line. For the skirt, cut two 16½" (41.8 cm) strips across the width of the fabric.

Ottoman

1 Using the yardstick, draw two lines across the wood circle, dividing in into equal fourths. Center a leg plate on each line 1½" (3.8 cm) from the circle edge. Mark the placement for the screw holes. Predrill the holes, using a drill bit slightly smaller than the screws. Screw a leg plate in place at each mark.

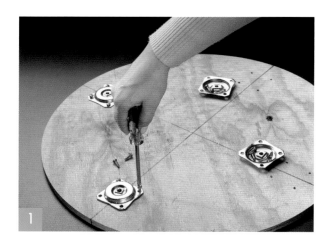

2 Secure the foam alternative to the top of the wood circle, using permanent fabric adhesive.

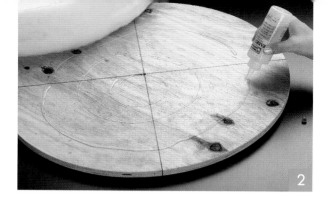

3 Place the fabric circle facedown on the work surface. Center the ottoman base, upside down over the fabric. Wrap the fabric edge tautly to the underside of the wood circle at two quarter marks and staple in place. Repeat at the other quarter marks. Check to be sure the fabric is stretched evenly at the four points.

4 Continue to wrap the fabric edge to the underside of the circle, spacing the staples close together. Trim the fabric edge ½" (1.3 cm) from the staples.

5 Pin the skirt strips right sides together along the short ends. Stitch ½" (1.3 cm) seams and press them open.

6 Finish the lower raw edge with serging or zigzag stitches. Press the edge under 1½" (3.8 cm) and topstitch in place.

Divide the upper edge of the skirt in fourths and mark with pins. Sew two rows of gathering stitches in the seam allowance between each set of pins.

7 Screw the legs into the leg plates. Slide the skirt over the ottoman base, aligning the pin marks with the legs; pin the skirt to the ottoman at the pin marks, with the top of the skirt 1" (2.5 cm) above the bottom of the wood base. Pull the threads to evenly gather each section. Pin the skirt to the ottoman, inserting pins straight into the foam just above the wood circle. Staple the skirt to the side of the wood; remove the pins. Trim the fabric just above the staples.

8 Apply fabric adhesive to the wrong side of the fringe header, and adhere the fringe to the upper edge of the skirt, covering the raw edge and staples.

Decorator Pillows

illows add a wonderful finishing touch to any décor, indoors or out. The fabric and trims shown here are designed for the outdoors, but the inserts are regular pillow forms. If they will be left outdoors during long periods of rain, cover the pillow form with a plastic bag before inserting it in the cover.

Part of the fun of sewing for your home is mixing and matching fabrics and trims, and pillows give you the chance to experiment without making a big investment. Choose coordinating prints in different sizes to combine with stripes, plaids, or checks.

While you're having fun selecting fabrics, don't forget the trims; they give any pillow a polished look. Trims can be stitched in place or adhered with permanent fabric adhesive or fusible web tape.

There are several ways to close the pillows. The square pillow has an overlapped closure held in place with hook-and-loop tape. The bolster pillow closes with an invisible zipper. Both closures make it easy to remove the cover for cleaning or to replace the insert. If you don't want to remove the cover, you can slip-stitch it closed.

MATERIALS FOR SQUARE PILLOW

- ⅝ yd. (0.6 m) indoor/outdoor decorator fabric, 54" (137 cm) wide

- ½ yd. (0.5 m) sew-on hook-and-loop tape

- 2¼ yd. (2.1 m) indoor/outdoor twisted cording with lip

- Masking or clear tape, ½" (1.3 cm) wide

- 18" (46 cm) pillow form

MATERIALS FOR BOLSTER

- ½ yd. (0.5 m) indoor/outdoor decorator fabric for center panel

- ¼ yd. (0.25 m) contrasting indoor/outdoor decorator fabric for ends

- 12" (30.5 cm) invisible zipper

- Invisible zipper presser foot

- 14" x 6" (35.5 x 15 cm) bolster pillow form

- 1¼ yd. (1.15 m) indoor/outdoor tassel fringe with decorative header

- Permanent fabric adhesive

Cutting Directions

For the square pillow, cut a 19" (48.5 cm) square for the front; for the back, cut two 19" x 11" (48.5 x 28 cm) rectangles. For the bolster, cut a 16" x 21" (40.5 x 53.5) rectangle for the center panel; from the contrasting fabric, cut two 7" (18 cm) circles for the ends.

Square Pillow with Twisted Cord Welting

1 Finish one long edge of each pillow back piece with serging or zigzag stitches. Center the hook side of the tape on the right side of one piece, ¼" (6 mm) from the finished edge. Stitch in place along both sides. Repeat with the loop side of the tape for the remaining pillow back.

2 Turn under the edge with the hook tape 1½" (3.8 cm) and stitch in place ¼" (6 mm) from the finished edge. Overlap the back pieces and press the tapes together. Baste across the ends of the overlap to form a 19" (48.5 cm) square.

3 Pin the twisted welting to the pillow back with the right sides of the fabric and welting facing up and the outer edge of the welting lip aligned to the raw edge of the fabric. Plan for the ends to overlap in the center of one side. Avoid extra bulk by not overlapping them at the closure. Clip into the welting lip at the corners. Using a zipper foot, stitch ½" (1.3 cm) from the edge. Leave 1½" (3.8 cm) unstitched between the ends; leave 3" (7.5 cm) tails.

4 Remove the stitches holding the welting to the lip on the tails. Trim the lip ends so they overlap 1" (2.5 cm). Separate the cord plies, and wrap the end of each ply with tape to prevent raveling. Arrange the plies so those on the right turn up and those on the left turn down.

(continued)

5 Insert the plies on the right under the crossed lip ends, twisting and pulling them down until the welting is returned to its original shape. Secure in place with tape.

6 Twist and pull the plies on the left over the plies on the right until the join looks like continuous twisted welting from both sides. Tape in place.

7 Position the zipper foot on the left of the needle, if possible. Place the pillow back to the right of the needle; this will allow you to stitch in the direction of the cord twists. Machine-baste through all layers to secure the welting. If you are unable to adjust your machine to stitch in this position, remove the presser foot and stitch manually over the thick cords. Be sure the presser foot lever is down so the thread tension is engaged.

8 Pin the pillow front to the pillow back, right sides together. With the pillow back facing up, stitch ½" (1.3 cm) from the edge, stitching just inside the basting stitches, crowding the welting.

9 Separate the hook-and-loop tapes and turn the pillow cover right side out. Insert the pillow form and close the cover.

Bolster Pillow

1 Open the zipper. Center the zipper along one long edge, right sides together, with the zipper coil aligned to the seamline. Pin in place. Finish the seam allowance, catching the zipper tape in the stitches.

2 Attach the invisible zipper foot to the machine; position the zipper coil under the appropriate groove of the foot. Stitch, starting at the top of the zipper until the zipper foot touches the pull tab at the bottom.

2

6 Pin a circle to one end, right sides together, aligning the raw edges. The cylinder ends will fan out at the clips. Stitch a ½" (1.3 cm) seam, keeping the outer edges even. Repeat at the opposite end.

6

3 Secure the other side of the zipper to the other long edge, as in step 1. Position the coil under the appropriate groove of the zipper foot. The bulk of the fabric will be on the opposite side of the needle. Stitch, starting at the top of the zipper until the zipper foot touches the pull tab at the bottom.

4 Close the zipper. Adjust the zipper foot to get as close as possible to the zipper. Stitch the rest of the seam above and below the zipper. Open the zipper partway.

5 Staystitch a scant ½" (1.3 cm) from the edge at each open end of the cylinder. Clip up to the stitching line every ½" (1.3 cm).

7 Open the zipper and turn the bolster cover right side out. Insert the pillow form and close the zipper.

8 Apply permanent fabric adhesive to the tassel fringe heading, and glue the trim, with fringe turned outward, to the ends of the bolster. Overlap the ends at the seamline.

OUTDOOR DINING

Round Tablecloth with Napkins

Set an elegant table when you make a round tablecloth that drops all the way to the ground. A set of fringed napkins finishes the look.

You will probably use a printed fabric, so be sure to buy enough that you can match the print. The tablecloth shown is 106" (269.5 cm) in diameter and fits a 48" (122 cm) diameter table with a 29" (73.5 cm) drop. The fabric used has a pattern repeat of 13" (33 cm), so 6 ⅓ yd. (5.8 m) of fabric was needed to match the design at the seams. To make the seams less conspicuous, a full fabric panel is used across the center of the tablecloth and a half-width panel is matched to it on each side.

MATERIALS

- Indoor/outdoor decorator fabric, 54" (137 cm) wide, amount determined in step 1

- Scissors or rotary cutter and mat

- Basting tape

- Yardstick or tape measure

- Pencil

- Fusible adhesive tape, ½" (1.3 cm) wide

- ⅔ yd. (0.63 m) even-weave cotton or linen fabric for two napkins

Round Tablecloth

1 Measure the diameter of the table; add twice the drop length to this measurement, plus 1" (2.5 cm) for a hem allowance to determine the cut diameter of the tablecloth. Purchase twice the length of the total measurement for fabric that doesn't need matching at the seams. For fabric with a printed design, add the length of one pattern repeat (see page 8) to the total measurement.

2 Cut the fabric in half crosswise; set one panel aside. Cut the remaining panel in half lengthwise. To match the print, press under the width of the seam allowances on the selvage sides of the half-width pieces. Match the print at the folds with the print at the selvages of the full-width piece. Use basting tape to adhere the matched layers together. Pin to prevent the weight of the layers from pulling away from the basting tape.

3 Sew the half panels to the sides of the full panel, stitching in the well of the fold. Trim off the selvages evenly. Finish the seam allowances together with serging or zigzag stitches.

4 Divide the cut diameter measurement in half to determine the radius of the tablecloth. Fold the fabric in half lengthwise, then crosswise. Pin the layers together. Using a tape measure and pencil, measure from the folded corner and mark an arc equal to the radius length, across the fabric. Cut through all layers along the marked line. Unfold the fabric.

5 Finish the outer raw edge with serging or zigzag stitches. Fuse the adhesive tape to the wrong side of the finished outer edge; do not remove the paper. Feeling the paper edge as a guide, press the edge under ½" (1.3 cm). Remove the paper backing and press the edge to fuse in place. From the right side, topstitch the hem to finish.

Fringed Napkins

1 For each napkin, cut a 22" (56 cm) square of fabric on the exact lengthwise and crosswise grains.

2 Stitch around the square 1" (2.5 cm) from the edge, using matching or contrasting thread.

3 Pull out the yarns parallel to the stitching on each side of the napkin to fringe the edges.

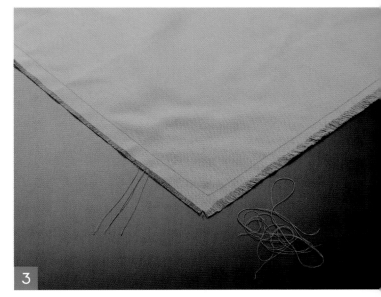

Tablecloths for Umbrella Tables

Round and oval tables with a center umbrella are found on lots of patios and decks. Here is a tablecloth that is constructed with a center hole for the umbrella's pole. A hook-and-loop tape closure extends from the center hole so you don't have to remove the umbrella when positioning the tablecloth. To keep the breeze from blowing the tablecloth up onto the table, drapery weights are stitched along the lower edge of the tablecloth.

For tablecloths with body, select firmly woven, medium-weight fabrics, such as poplin or denim. It is often necessary to seam two or more lengths of fabric together for the desired width. If the fabric width being added to the full fabric width is 10" (25.5 cm) or narrower, stitch the additional fabric width to one side of the full fabric width; the seam falls within the drop length of the tablecloth and is not noticeable. If the additional width needed is more than 10"

(25.5 cm), use a full fabric width in the center and stitch equal narrow panels to the sides.

MATERIALS

- Indoor/outdoor decorator fabric

- Pencil

- Yardstick

- Scrap of nonwoven interfacing

- Hook-and-loop tape, ¾" (2 cm) wide

- Plastic-covered drapery weights

Cutting Directions

For a round table, measure the diameter of the table; add 20" (51 cm) to determine the measurement for the finished tablecloth. This allows for a 10" (25.5 cm) drop length or overhang. Cut a square of fabric 1" (2.5 cm) larger than this size; piece two fabric widths together, if necessary, and press the seams open.

For an oval table, measure the center length and width of the table; add 20" (51 cm) to each measurement to determine the dimensions for the finished tablecloth; this allows for a 10" (25.5 cm) drop length or overhang. Cut a rectangle of fabric 1" (2.5 cm) larger than this size; piece two fabric widths together, if necessary, and press the seams open.

Round Tablecloth

1 Fold the square of fabric in half lengthwise, then crosswise. Pin the layers together. Divide the measurement for the finished tablecloth by two and add ¼" (6 mm) to determine the radius of the cut circle. Using a pencil, mark an arc, measuring from the folded center of the fabric, a distance equal to the radius.

3 Cut on the marked lines through all the layers. Cut along one folded edge; this will be the opening of the tablecloth.

4 Cut two 3" (7.5 cm) strips of fabric for the placket opening, with the length of each strip equal to the cut length of the tablecloth opening plus 1" (2.5 cm).

5 Cut an 8" (20.5 cm) fabric square for the facing; fold the square in half lengthwise, then crosswise. Mark an arc, measuring 3" (7.5 cm) from the folded center of the fabric. Mark a second arc 1" (2.5 cm) from the folded center.

(continued)

2 Mark another arc 1" (2.5 cm) from the folded center of the fabric.

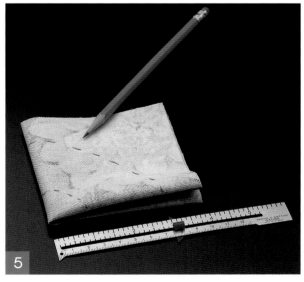

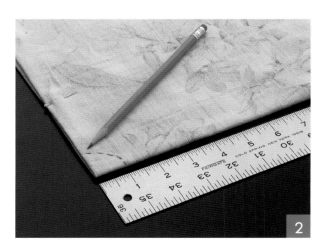

6 Cut the fabric on the marked lines; cut along one folded edge.

7 Use serging or zigzag stitching to finish the outer curved edge of the facing. Pin the facing to the tablecloth, right sides together and raw edges even. Stitch a ¼" (6 mm) seam around the center of the facing. Clip the seam allowances.

8 Press the seam allowances toward the facing. Understitch by stitching on the right side of the facing, close to the seamline. Press the facing to the underside of the tablecloth.

9 Press under a scant ½" (1.3 cm) on one long edge of the placket. Pin the placket to the opening edge of the tablecloth, with the right sides together and raw edges even; extend the placket ends ½" (1.3 cm) beyond the edges of the tablecloth. Stitch a ½" (1.3 cm) seam.

10 Press the seam allowances toward the placket. Fold the placket right sides together, with the folded edge of the placket extending a scant ⅛" (3 mm) beyond the seamline; pin. Using a piece of paper folded in quarters, mark an arc 1 ¼" (3.2 cm) from the folded center; cut on the marked line. Unfold the paper pattern to make a circle. Using the circle pattern, mark a curved seamline on the placket. Stitch on the marked line; trim the seam.

11 Turn the placket right side out, with the pressed edge of the placket just covering the seam on the back of the tablecloth; pin. Stitch in the ditch on the tablecloth top by stitching over the seamline in the well of the seam; catch the placket on the back of the tablecloth in the stitching.

12 Trim the ends of the placket even with the outer edge of the tablecloth. Apply the second placket to the remaining opening edge, following steps 9 to 11.

(continued)

13 Finish the raw edge of the tablecloth with serging or zigzag stitches. Press under the fabric ¼" (6 mm) from the edge. Machine-stitch the hem in place.

14 Cut the hook-and-loop tape into 1" (2.5 cm) strips. Pin the hook side of the tape to the overlap, centering the tape on the placket; stitch around the tape. Pin the loop side of the tape to the placket underlap, directly under the hook side of the tape; stitch. Repeat to position the hook-and-loop tape at about 6" (15 cm) intervals.

15 Secure drapery weights along the lower edge of the tablecloth at about 24" (61 cm) intervals; reinforce the fabric at the stitching lines with small pieces of firm, nonwoven interfacing.

Oval Tablecloth

1 Fold the fabric square in half lengthwise, then crosswise. Pin the layers together. Follow steps 2 to 12 on pages 61 to 63; in step 3, cut along one of the short folded edges.

2 Place the tablecloth on the table; weight the fabric down. Measure and mark around the tablecloth an amount equal to the desired drop length plus ¼" (6 mm). Cut on the marked line.

3 Complete the tablecloth as in steps 13 to 15, opposite.

Rectangular Tablecloth with Tied Corners

Tablecloths for rectangular or square tables are quick to make. This style has a unique design feature at the corners that helps to hold the tablecloth in place. Grommets and leather lacing tied through decorative metal conchos cinch the cloth together. You can use buttonholes instead of grommets. This tablecloth style is also useful on card tables set up for outdoor entertaining.

For durable tablecloths, select firmly woven fabrics, such as poplin or denim that can be easily laundered. It is often necessary to seam two lengths of fabric together for the desired width. If the panel being added to the full fabric width is 10" (25.5 cm) or narrower, stitch the panel to one side of the full fabric width; the seam falls within the drop length or overhang of the tablecloth and will not be noticeable. If the panel is wider than 10" (25.5 cm), use the full fabric width in the center and stitch narrower side panels to both sides; this positions the seams evenly on each side of the table.

MATERIALS

- Fabric

- Size 0 or ¼" (6 mm) grommets; attaching tool

- 2½ yd. (2.3 m) braided lacing or ribbon

- Craft wire, for securing ends of lacing

- Four conchos (optional)

Cutting Directions

Measure the length and width of the table. Add 20" (51 cm) to each measurement to determine the dimensions of the finished tablecloth; this allows for a 10" (25.5 cm) drop length, or overhang. Cut a rectangle of fabric 1" (2.5 cm) larger than this size; piece the fabric widths together, if necessary, and press the seams open.

Tablecloth

1 Press under ½" (1.3 cm) on each side of the fabric. Unfold the corner; fold diagonally so the pressed folds match. Press the diagonal fold; trim the corner as shown.

2 Fold under the raw edge ¼" (6 mm). Press the double-fold hem in place.

3 Stitch the hem close to the inner fold, pivoting at the corners; do not stitch along the folds of the miter.

4 Place the tablecloth on the table; pin-mark the grommet placement about 3" (7.5 cm) in from the corner of the table and 5" (12.7 cm) below the upper edge of the table. Repeat at the opposite side of the corner and at the remaining three corners to mark for eight grommets.

5 Attach the grommets securely, following the manufacturer's directions.

6 Reposition the tablecloth. Cut the braided lacing into four equal lengths; wrap the ends with craft wire or tie the ends in knots. Insert the lacing through the grommets at each corner, and secure a concho or tie a knot, cinching the fabric. If the table style allows, wrap the lacing behind a table leg for a more secure placement.

Retro
Oilcloth Placemats

Create a fun retro look in your outdoor dining with oilcloth placemats edged in giant rickrack. Colorful and easy to make, these placemats can be easily cleaned with a wipe of a damp cloth.

Oilcloth was once made by soaking fabric in linseed oil and varnish to make it waterproof. Modern oilcloth is actually vinyl-coated fabric or printed vinyl sealed to a woven base to give it more stability. A popular and practical fabric, vinyl oilcloth is now available in many bold, colorful prints and solids. The materials listed make two placemats.

Cutting Directions

Cut two 14" x 19" (35.5 x 48.5 cm) rectangles from the oilcloth.

Oilcloth Placemat

1 Cut two 19" (48.5 cm) lengths and two 14" (35.5 cm) lengths of rickrack. Begin and end each length at the same point on the rickrack curve. Apply seam sealant to the cut ends to prevent raveling.

2 Apply basting tape along one long edge on the right side of the placemat. Peel back the paper backing from one end. Position the rickrack along the edge of the placemat with the peaks extending ½" (1.3 cm) beyond the edge.

3 Baste the rickrack in place ⅜" (1 cm) from the edge of the placemat.

4 Fold the rickrack to the back along the basting line. Topstitch ⅜" (1 cm) from the edge of the placemat. Stitch again halfway between the topstitching line and the edge.

5 Repeat steps 2 through 4 to finish the remaining long edge; then repeat to finish the short edges.

6 On the wrong side of the placemat, use fabric adhesive to glue the overlapping corners in place as needed to lie flat.

OUTDOOR FUN
AND RELAXATION

Colorful Hammock

where better to spend your relaxation time than in a hammock in your own backyard? This style is not only comfortable but decorative, made from a bold decorator print fabric with an inner layer of sturdy canvas. If you want to be able to leave your hammock outdoors, be sure to use indoor/outdoor decorator fabric and canvas. Closet-pole rods and nylon rope support the hammock. The instructions make a hammock bed 49" x 77" (125 x 195.6 cm).

Metal rings are secured to each end, so the hammock can be easily hung on a purchased hammock frame. You can also tie the hammock between the trunks of two trees with additional lengths of rope secured to the metal rings.

MATERIALS

- 2¾ yd. (2.55 m) outer fabric, 54" (137 cm) wide

- 2¾ yd. (2.55 m) heavy-duty canvas, 54" (137 cm) wide, for lining

- Two 50" (127 cm) lengths of hardwood closet pole, 1¼" (3.2 cm) in diameter

- Pencil

- Clamp

- Scrap lumber

- Drill and ½" spade bit

- Exterior primer; exterior paint

- 40 ft. (12.2 m) braided nylon rope, ⅜" (1 cm) in diameter; bodkin

- Bodkin

- Masking tape

- Two #2 x 2" (5 cm) steel rings

Cutting Directions

Cut one 53" x 78" (134.5 x 198 cm) rectangle from the outer fabric, trimming the selvages. Cut one 52" x 78" (132 x 198 cm) rectangle from the canvas lining, trimming the selvages. For the pole sleeves, cut two 8" x 45" (20.5 x 115 cm) rectangles from both the outer fabric and the lining.

Hammock

1 Pin the outer fabric and lining for one pole sleeve, right sides together, matching the raw edges. Stitch ½" (1.3 cm) seams at the short ends. Repeat for the remaining pole sleeve.

2 Press the seam allowances open. Turn the sleeve right side out; press. Fold one pole sleeve in half lengthwise, wrong sides together; pin along the raw edges. Repeat for the remaining pole sleeve.

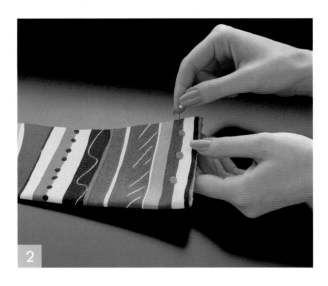

3 Pin-mark the center of each pole sleeve; pin-mark the center of the hammock outer fabric at the upper and lower edges. Pin one sleeve to the right side of the hammock outer fabric at each end, matching pin marks and raw edges; the outer fabric extends beyond the sleeves at the sides. Machine-baste a scant ½" (1.3 cm) from the raw edges.

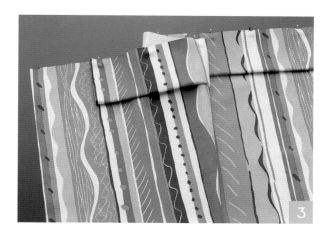

4 Pin the hammock lining and outer fabric, right sides together, along the upper and lower edges; center the lining so the outer fabric extends ½" (1.3 cm) beyond the lining at the sides. Stitch ½" (1.3 cm) seams.

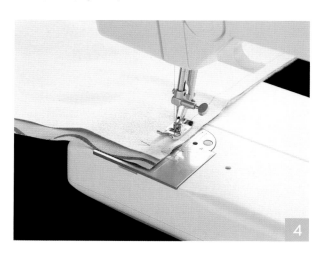

5 Turn the hammock right side out; press. Topstitch ⅛" and ⅜" (3 mm and 1 cm) from the seam.

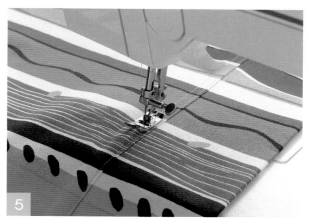

6 Place the hammock on a flat surface, lining side up. Pin the fabric and lining together at the sides, 5" (12.7 cm) from the raw edges of the outer fabric.

7 Press up ½" (1.3 cm) on the long edges of the outer fabric, encasing the edges of the lining. Then press the outer fabric and lining up 1½" (3.8 cm); pin.

(continued)

8 Stitch close to the folded edge to make the casing; stitch again ¼" (6 mm) from the first row of stitching.

9 Hold the pole firmly against the table; using a pencil placed flat on the table, draw a line on the pole.

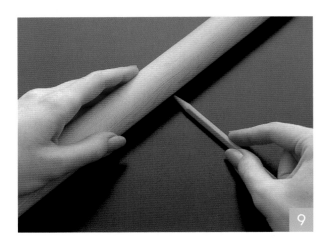

10 Mark a point on the line 1" (2.5 cm) from each end. Clamp the pole to the work surface, placing a scrap of lumber under the pole at the marking. Using a ½" (1.3 cm) spade bit and placing the point of the bit at the mark, drill a hole; repeat at the opposite end. Drill holes at the ends of the remaining pole.

11 Apply primer to the poles, applying two coats at the ends. Paint the poles as desired.

12 Cut the rope in half; wrap the ends with masking tape to prevent raveling. Using a bodkin, thread the rope through the side casing, with the ends extending evenly. Repeat to thread the rope through the opposite casing.

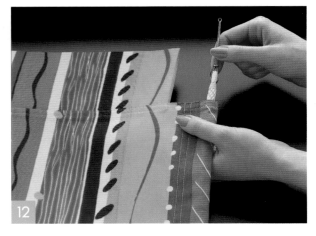

13 Spread the hammock on a flat surface. Insert a pole into each rod sleeve. Tie an overhand knot 1½" (3.8 cm) beyond the end of the casing. Thread the rope through the hole in the pole, and push the pole firmly against the knot. Tie a second overhand knot to secure the pole. Repeat at each corner of the hammock, making sure there is no slack in the rope.

14 Secure the ropes to metal rings for hanging the hammock; the length of the ropes depends on the distance between the hammock frame ends or trees. Mark dots on the ropes at the desired length. Secure one rope at one end of the hammock to a ring, using a fisherman's bend knot as shown in the following two photos.

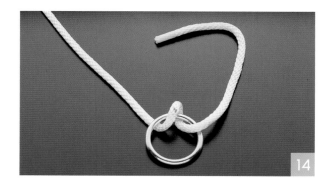

15 Secure the free end of the rope with two half hitches as shown. Secure the remaining rope at this end of the hammock; then secure the ropes to the ring at the opposite end of the hammock.

16 Hang the hammock on the hammock frame or secure it to trees, using an additional length of rope.

Fanciful Hanging Cabana

H ang this breezy cabana from a tree branch; then set a bench or chairs inside for a fairy-tale setting. It features a topper of waterproof canvas accented with outdoor trims. A purchased mosquito netting canopy hangs from a large wicker ring, available at import and linen stores.

You can fan out the netting into a wide circle and hold it in place with a few small rocks. Or part the netting and sweep it to the sides to create a dreamy retreat. If the insects start to bite, draw the netting closed.

MATERIALS

- Pattern paper

- String

- Sharp pencil

- Yardstick

- 2 yd. (1.85 m) striped outdoor canvas, 32" (81.5 cm) wide

- 2¼ yd. (2.1 m) solid-color outdoor canvas, 32" (81.5 cm) wide

- Metal ring, 1¾" (4.5 cm) diameter

- Paper clips

- 2¼ yd. (2.1 m) indoor/outdoor brush fringe

- 4½ yd. (4.15 m) indoor/outdoor tassel fringe with decorative header

- 3 yd. (2.75 m) grosgrain ribbon or twill tape, ¼" (6 mm) wide

- Mosquito netting canopy with 25½" (64.8 cm) diameter ring

Cutting Directions

Cut four striped pieces for the cabana topper using the pattern drawn in steps 1 and 2. Align the center line of the pattern to the center of a stripe in the fabric. Cut a 10" x 81" (25.5 x 206 cm) strip of solid-color canvas for the cabana border. Cut a 1" x 3" (2.5 x 7.5 cm) strip of the canvas for a hanging loop.

Hanging Cabana

1 Place the pattern paper on a surface that can be pinned into and mark a dot for the triangle top. Tie one end of a piece of string around a pencil. Measure 22½" (57.3 cm) from the pencil and insert a pin through the string at this point. Insert the pin through the marked point on the paper. Holding the string taut, draw an arc 21" (53.5 cm) wide (to fit a ring with a 25½" (64.8 cm) diameter). If your ring diameter is different, measure the outer diameter of the ring. Multiply the diameter by 3.14 to determine the circumference. Divide the circumference by 4 to determine the base width of the arc; add 1" (2.5 cm) to the width for seam allowances. Draw the pattern using this measurement at the base. Note: a wider arc will result in a shorter canopy; a narrower arc will result in a taller canopy.

2 Draw a line to connect each end of the arc to the top mark, using a yardstick. Also draw a line from the top mark to the center of the arc. Cut out the pattern and use it to cut four cabana sections from the striped fabric.

3 Sew two cabana sections together using ½" (1.3 cm) seams and matching the stripes. Press the seam allowances open with your fingers and topstitch the seam allowances in place. Repeat for the other two sections.

4 Fold the long edges of the hanging loop to the center and stitch ¼" (6 mm) from each fold. Fold the strip in half through the metal ring, and center it at the upper point of one cabana topper unit; hold it in place with a paper clip.

(continued)

5 Sew the two topper units, right sides together. At the upper point, stitch straight across, catching the loop ends in the stitches. Stitch across the point several times to ensure the loop is secure. Finger-press the seam allowance open and topstitch as close as possible to the point.

6 Machine-baste the brush fringe to the lower edge of the cabana topper, right sides together, with the fringe header aligned to the fabric edge.

7 To make the band for a 25½"-diameter (64.8 cm) ring, enlarge the pattern on page 112 and cut it out. Aligning the baseline of the pattern to one long edge of the cabana border strip, trace the pattern four times continuously, overlapping the pieces on the dotted seamline; leave ½" (1.3 cm) seam allowances on the outer edges of the first and last points. Cut out the border. To make the band for a different ring size, adjust the base of the triangles on the band pattern to fit the circumference.

8 Stitch the tassel fringe to the shaped edge of the border, aligning the lower edge of the header to the fabric edge. Stitch along both edges of the header, folding small tucks at the points and inner corners so the trim lays flat.

9 Stitch the short ends of the border together. Pin or paper clip the border to the edge of the topper, right sides together, positioning two border points between the seamlines of each section. Stitch together ½" (1.3 cm) from the raw edges, enclosing the brush fringe header. Turn the seam allowances toward the top and topstitch in place.

10 Cut eight 12" (30.5 cm) lengths of ribbon. On the wrong side of the topper, mark eight evenly spaced tie placements just above the lower edge seam allowances. Fold each ribbon length in half and sew the center to a placement mark, stitching back and forth across the ribbon several times.

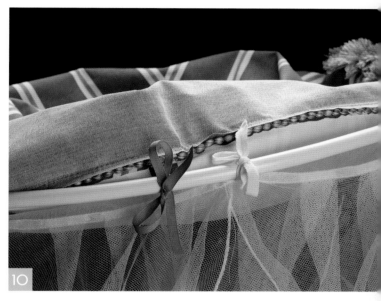

11 Tie the mosquito netting canopy to the large wicker ring, with the top of the canopy beneath the ring. Tie the topper onto the ring using the ribbon ties.

Deluxe Picnic Quilt

This tufted and padded quilt is perfect for a picnic or lounging on your lawn. The colorful indoor/outdoor decorator fabric on the face of the quilt resists stains and fading. The wipe-clean vinyl backing is waterproof, making it ideal for dry or damp ground. Polyester batting gives the quilt comfortable loft.

Spread out your quilt for an instant backyard dining space or a place for the kids to stretch out and read a book.

A fabric wrap with handles makes it easy to store the quilt or take it along to a park or the beach.

MATERIALS

- Medium-loft polyester batting for full-size quilt

- 2½ yd. (2.3 m) indoor/outdoor decorator fabric

- 2 yd. (1.85 m) lightweight vinyl

- Permanent fabric adhesive

- Disappearing fabric marker

- Coordinating yarn

- Sharp, large-eye needle

- ⅓ yd (0.32 m) hook-and-loop tape, ¾" (2 cm) wide

- 2½ yd. (2.3 m) nylon strapping, 1" (2.5 cm) wide

- Candle and match

Cutting Directions

Cut one 54" x 72" (137 x 183 cm) rectangle each from the decorator fabric and vinyl; trim off the selvages. Cut one 54" x 72" (137 x 183 cm) rectangle from the batting. For the quilt wrap, cut two 11" x 28" (28 x 71 cm) rectangles from decorator fabric and one from the batting.

Picnic Quilt

1 Place the batting on the wrong side of the fabric and trim it even with the fabric edges. Machine-baste the edges of the batting and fabric together.

2 Pin the decorator fabric and vinyl right sides together, pinning ¼" (6 mm) from the edges. Sew together, using a ½" (1.3 cm) seam allowance and leaving a 12" (30.5 cm) opening for turning on one short edge.

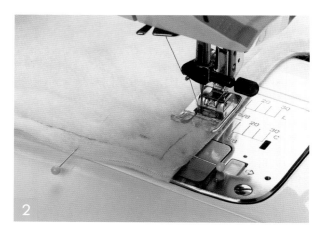

3 Trim the corners diagonally. Turn the quilt right side out. Turn the opening seam allowances under and use fabric adhesive to glue the edges together.

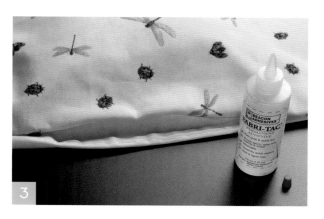

4 Use your fingers to press the edges to crease; do not press with an iron. Topstitch ¼" (6 mm) from the edges.

5 Mark the quilt top for tufting in four evenly spaced rows of three marks each, using a fabric marker.

6 Thread the needle with a double strand of yarn. Working from the right side of the quilt, make a ¼" (6 mm) stitch through all the layers at a mark. Leave a 1½" (3.8 cm) tail of yarn. Knot the yarn tight against the quilt surface and trim the tails evenly. Repeat at each mark, rethreading the needle when the yarn gets too short.

7 Place the fabric layers for the quilt wrap right sides together and place the batting on top. Stitch with the batting on top, leaving an opening in one short end for turning. Trim the corners diagonally. Turn the wrap right side out and press. Press the opening seam allowances under and pin closed. Topstitch ¼" (6 mm) from the edges all around the wrap.

8 Cut a 9½" (24.3 cm) length of the hook-and-loop tape and separate the strips. Sew the loop strip across one short end of the wrap, ¼" (6 mm) from the end. Turn the wrap over and sew the hook strip 2" (5 cm) from the other end.

9 Seal the cut ends of the nylon strapping by holding them close to a candle flame. Allow them to cool. Overlap the ends 1" (2.5 cm) and stitch along both edges with a zigzag stitch, forming the strap into a circle.

10 Center the strap circle on the wrap 1" (2.5 cm) from each side of the wrap; the loop ends should extend evenly beyond the ends of the wrap. Pin the strap in place, placing the first and last pins on each side 3½" (9 cm) from the short ends of the wrap. Sew the strap to the wrap, sewing along both edges between the first and last pins. Zigzag back and forth across the strap at the ends of the stitching lines to secure.

Nylon Privacy Screen

Divide your outdoor space into a cozy, secluded area for sunbathing, napping, or entertaining with a lightweight nylon privacy screen. Made of colorful ripstop nylon and PVC pipes, this screen is easy to set up and take down whenever and wherever it is needed. The PVC pipes, which fit into casings sewn in the screen, are pushed into the ground for easy setup. For carrying and storing the screen, simply roll it up and secure it with the handy ties.

PVC pipes, available at home improvement stores, are inexpensive, lightweight, and easy to cut. Though ripstop nylon does not

have a right or wrong side, select one side and use it consistently as the right side when sewing the hems and casings.

MATERIALS

- 4 yd. (3.7 m) ripstop nylon fabric, 60" (152.5 cm) wide

- Clear quilter's ruler or yardstick

- Water-soluble fabric marker

- Fusible adhesive tape, ½" (1.3 cm) wide

- Basting tape

- Pressing cloth

- 2 yd. (1.85 m) nylon strapping, 1" (2.5 cm) wide

- Candle and match

- Four PVC pipes, 72" (183 cm) long, ½" (1.3 cm) diameter

Screen

1 Straighten the cut ends of the fabric. Turn the fabric so the selvages are at the top and bottom. Beginning at the left edge, mark the upper and lower edges into segments as follows: 5", 38½", 5", 38½", 5", 38½", 5" (12.7, 98, 12.7, 98, 12.7, 98, 12.7 cm). Repeat to mark across the center of the fabric. Use the yardstick and fabric marker to draw straight lines between the upper and lower edges at the marks.

2 Apply fusible adhesive tape along the right side of one long edge; do not remove the paper backing. Fold the edge to the wrong side ½" (1.3 cm) then ½" (1.3 cm) again, using the paper backing as a guide. Press the folds, using a pressing cloth to protect the nylon. Lift the fold, remove the paper backing.

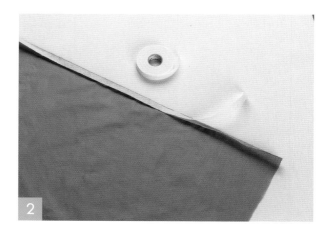

3 Refold the hem and fuse it in place. Topstitch ¼" (6 mm) from the bottom fold.

4 To make each end pocket, press the side edge under 2 ½" (6.5 cm), aligning the edge with the marked line; then press under again along the marked line. Secure the folded edge in place with basting tape.

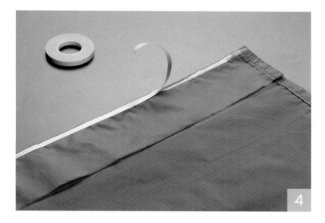

5 Stitch the folded edge in place ¼" (6 mm) from the inner edge. Repeat for the opposite short end.

6 To make each center pocket, bring the lines marked 5" (12.7 cm) apart together and use basting tape to secure. Press the folds. Topstitch ¼" (6 mm) from the fold on the right side. Then turn the fabric over and topstitch ¼" (6 mm) from the fold on the wrong side.

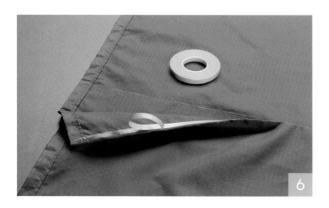

7 Follow steps 2 and 3 to hem the upper edge.

8 Cut the nylon strapping in half and seal the ends by holding them close to a candle flame. On one short end of the screen, measure 18" (46 cm) from the long edge and sew the center of a nylon strap to the inside pocket stitching line. Repeat for the other end.

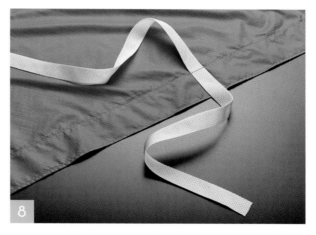

9 Insert a PVC pipe in each pocket. To stand the screen, insert the excess pipe length in the ground.

Decorative Flags

Decorative flags add a splash of color to your landscape. They add a festive touch to celebrations such as birthdays or barbeques and serve as easy-to-spot markers for guests. These flags are made using a reversible appliqué technique, so the design of the flag is visible from both sides. Select simple designs like those shown here. Patterns for these flag appliqués are on pages 110 and 111. You can also create your own appliqués by drawing the shapes or enlarging copyright-free illustrations.

For a flag that hangs well and can withstand several seasons of outdoor use, select a heavyweight nylon fabric, such as 200-denier nylon. This heavier fabric is especially easy to handle when applying appliqués using the reversible technique.

If you will be hanging the flag from a flagpole, select a pole that has a screw or clip at the end of the staff. This allows you to fasten a

small tab on the flag to the pole, which prevents the flag from shifting downward. Flags can be made in any size. A popular size for flags displayed on flagpoles is 28" x 40" (71 x 102 cm).

MATERIALS

- 200-denier nylon fabric for flag and appliqué pieces

- Appliqué pattern

- Liquid fray preventer

- Monofilament nylon thread; machine embroidery thread

- Chalk or water-soluble marking pen

- Appliqué scissors

- Water-soluble stabilizer

- Paper towels

- ¼" (6 mm) grosgrain ribbon, for streamers, optional

- Flagpole and mounting bracket for flagpole, or wood pole set

Decorative Flag

1 Cut the flag from the background fabric, adding 2" (5 cm) to the desired finished width and 5" (12.7 cm) to the desired finished length; this allows for hems and the upper casing. Cut appliqués in the desired shapes and colors.

2 Cut one 1" x 4" (2.5 x 10 cm) rectangle for the tab from the background fabric, if the flag will be hung from a flagpole; apply liquid fray preventer to the raw edges. Fold the fabric in half crosswise; stitch a ½" (1.3 cm) buttonhole about ¼" (6 mm) from the folded edge as shown. Set aside.

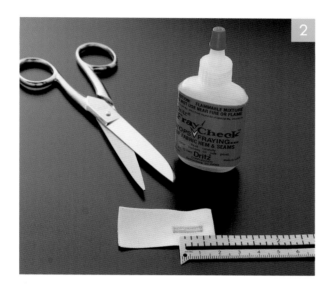

3 Press under ½" (1.3 cm) twice on one long edge of the flag. Straight-stitch close to the first fold, using monofilament thread. Repeat to hem the opposite long edge.

4 Press under ½" (1.3 cm) on the upper edge of the flag; then press under 3" (7.5 cm), for the casing. For a flag with a tab, center the tab on the foldline of the casing, on the wrong side of fabric, with the folded edge of the tab about ⅛" (3 mm) from the hemmed edge. Stitch in place as shown.

5 Fold the casing in place; pin. Stitch close to the first fold; then stitch ¼" (6 mm) above the first row of stitching.

6 Press under ½" (1.3 cm) at the lower edge of the flag; then press under 1" (2.5 cm). Pin in place. Stitch close to both folded edges; then stitch another row, centered between the previous stitching.

(continued)

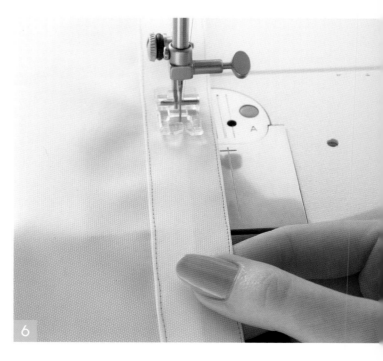

7 Position the appliqué pieces on the flag, and pin in place. For a layered design, pin the first layer only and mark the placement of the foreground layers, using a water-soluble marking pen or chalk.

8 Straight-stitch around the appliqué piece, about ⅛" (3 mm) from the raw edges, using monofilament thread.

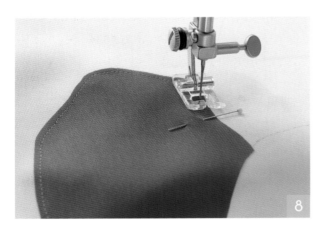

9 Separate the fabric layers, working from the back of the flag; trim away the background fabric, close to the stitching.

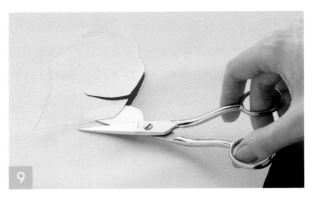

10 Repeat steps 8 and 9 for each background appliqué piece, then for any foreground appliqué pieces.

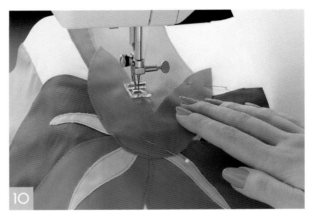

11 Cut water-soluble stabilizer about 2" (5 cm) larger than the area to be appliquéd. With the back of the flag facing up, position the stabilizer over the appliqué area; pin in place.

12 Set the machine for a short, wide zigzag stitch; use machine embroidery thread in the needle and bobbin. Satin-stitch around the appliqués, covering the raw edges of the fabric on the front and back of the flag; stitch the background appliqués first, then the foreground appliqués.

13 Mark any detail lines, such as veins of leaves or flowers, using chalk or water-soluble marking pen. Stitch, tapering the zigzag stitching at the ends by using narrower stitches.

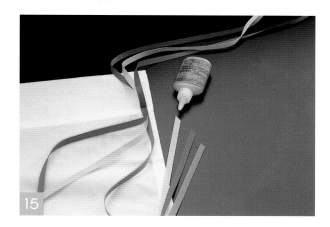

14 Trim excess stablizer from the back of the flag. Mist any remaining stabilizer with water to dissolve it; wipe the flag with an absorbent paper towel.

15 Stitch ribbon streamers to the upper corner of the flag, if desired, stitching over the previous stitching of the casing. Apply liquid fray preventer to the ribbon ends to prevent fraying. Hang the flag.

Design Extending off the Edge

1 Follow step 1, cutting the appliqué pieces so they extend to the raw edge of the background fabric. Continue as in steps 2 to 7, except do not stitch the hems and casing in place.

2 Stitch the appliqués as in steps 8 to 10, unpinning the hems and casing as necessary. Complete the flag as in steps 11 to 14. Stitch the hems and casing in place.

Windsocks

Windsocks with bright appliqués are decorative accents for yards or decks. Make a windsock that can be used year-round, or make several for the seasons.

Sewn from nylon fabric, a windsock can withstand sunlight, rain, and other weather conditions without fading or deteriorating. Lightweight nylons, such as ripstop and nylon broadcloth, are used because they catch the wind easily. To allow the windsock to turn freely in the breeze without tangling, it is hung with sturdy nylon cording or fishline attached to a swivel.

A fusible appliqué technique is used for sewing windsocks, making it easy to stitch the appliqués on lightweight nylon without puckering. Use the appliqué patterns on pages 108 and 109 to sew the windsocks shown here, or enlarge designs from coloring books or gift-wrapping paper to use as patterns for the appliqués.

MATERIALS

- ½ yd. (0.5 m) nylon fabric, for body of windsock and tails

- ¼ yd. (0.25 m) nylon fabric in one or two colors, for appliqués and tails

- Paper-backed fusible web

- Fabric marker or chalk

- 19" (48.5 cm) length of heavy-weight covered wire

- Waterproof vinyl tape

- Large-eye needle

- 1 yd. (0.92 m) nylon cording or monofilament nylon fishline for hanging windsock

- Windsock swivel or #5 or #6 ball-bearing fishing swivel to be used as hanger

Cutting Directions

Cut one 16½" x 18½" (41.8 x 47.3 cm) rectangle from the ½ yd. (0.5 m) piece of fabric for the body of the windsock. Cut a total of six tails, 3¼" x 22" (8.2 x 56 cm) each, on the crosswise grain, cutting two or three tails from each color of fabric as desired.

As in steps 1 and 2, opposite, cut the appliqués in the desired shapes and colors, using the remaining fabric.

Windsock

1 Trace the desired appliqué shapes onto the paper side of fusible web; for asymmetrical designs, trace the mirror image. Apply fusible web to the wrong side of the fabric, following the manufacturer's instructions.

2 Cut the appliqué pieces, following the marked lines on the fusible web; remove the paper backing.

3 Arrange the appliqué pieces on the body of the windsock, allowing for ¼" (6 mm) seams at the side and lower edges and a 1" (2.5 cm) casing at the top. Fuse the appliqués in place.

4 Mark any lines for design details. Stitch around the appliqués and along the marked lines, using short zigzag stitches of medium width.

5 Turn the long edges of the tails ¼" (6 mm) to the wrong side; stitch close to the fold. Trim the excess fabric close to the stitching.

(continued)

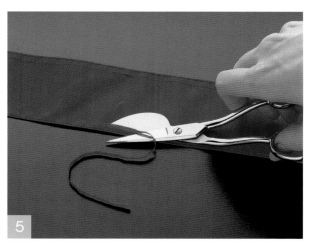

6 Turn the long edges to the wrong side again, enclosing the raw edge. Stitch over the previous stitches.

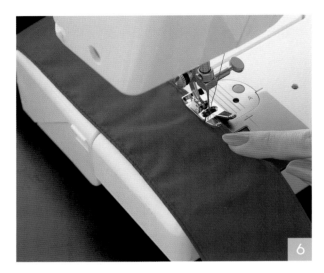

7 Fold the lower end of the tail in half, right sides together. Stitch a ¼" (6 mm) seam across the end. Press the seam open. Turn the end of the tail right side out, to form a point; press. Stitch and turn the remaining tail ends.

8 Pin the tails evenly along the lower edge of the windsock, with right sides together and raw edges even; leave ¼" (6 mm) seam allowance on the sides of the body. Stitch a ¼" (6 mm) seam along the lower edge; finish the seam, using serging or a zigzag stitches.

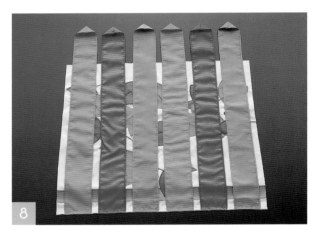

9 Turn the seam toward the windsock body, with the tails extending down. Topstitch the seam in place.

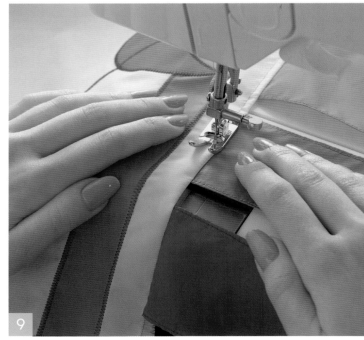

10 Fold the windsock body in half, matching raw edges at the side; stitch a ¼" (6 mm) seam. Finish the seam with serging or zigzag stitches. Turn the windsock right side out.

11 Press under ¼" (6 mm) on the upper edge of the windsock. Then press under ¾" (2 cm); pin in place to form a casing. Stitch close to the first fold; leave a 2" (5 cm) opening for inserting the wire.

12 Insert a 19" (48.5 cm) length of covered wire into the casing. Wrap the overlapped ends of wire together with waterproof tape to secure. Stitch the opening in the casing closed.

13 Divide the top of the windsock into thirds; mark. At each mark, take a single stitch through the casing, just below the wire, using a large-eye needle and a 12" (30.5 cm) length of nylon cording or fishline.

14 Tie the end of the nylon cording or fishline securely to the windsock.

15 Hold the ends of the cords together, keeping the lengths equal. Thread the ends through the eye of the ball-bearing swivel; tie securely. Hang the windsock.

Patterns

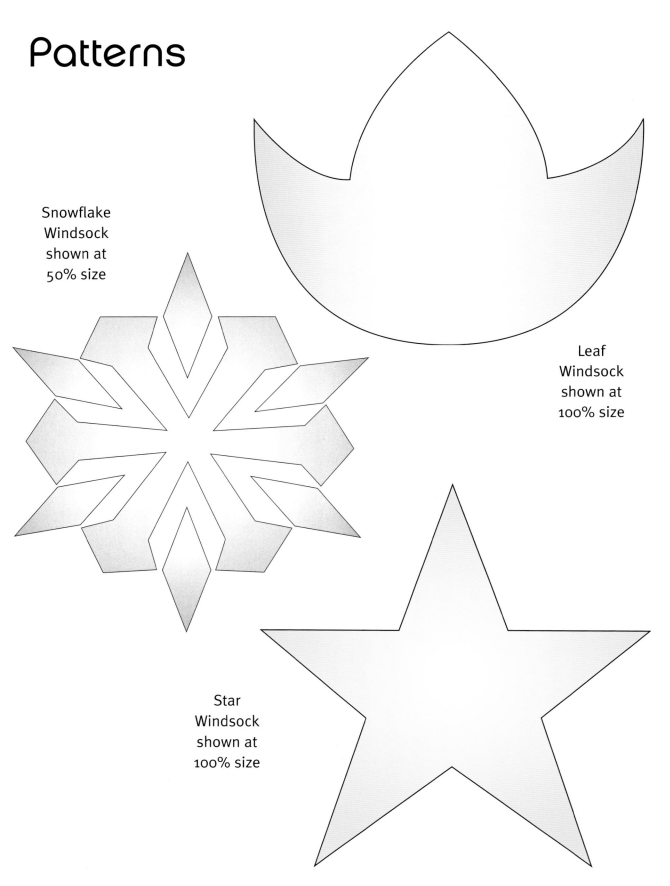

Snowflake
Windsock
shown at
50% size

Leaf
Windsock
shown at
100% size

Star
Windsock
shown at
100% size

Tulips
Windsock
shown at
50% size

8

9

5

1

3

4

7

2

6

Iris Flag
shown at
25% size

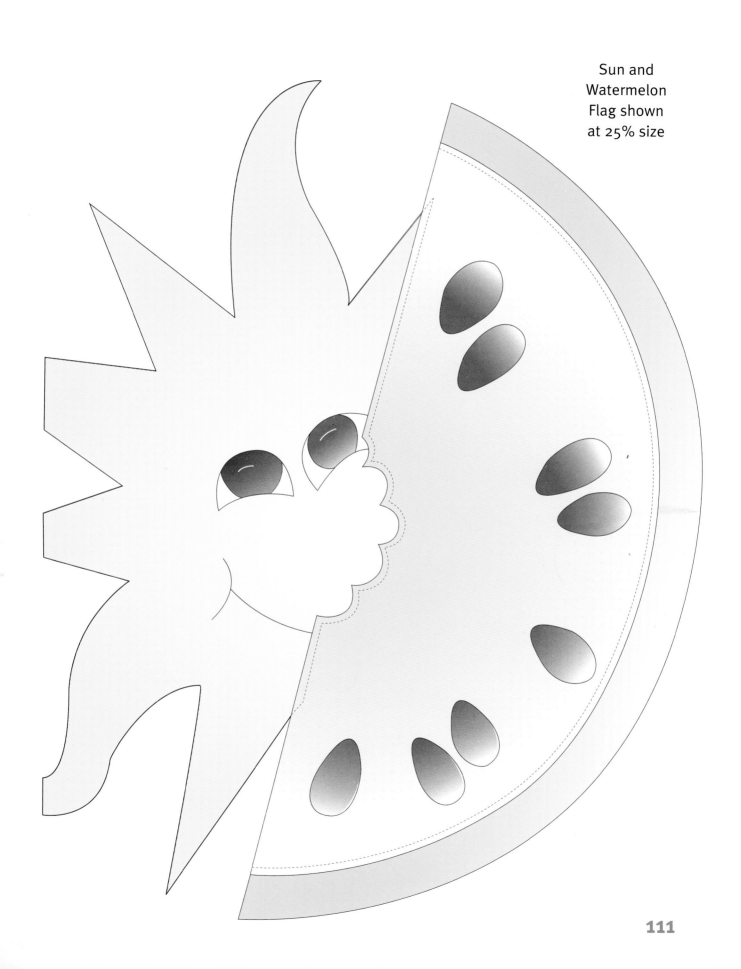

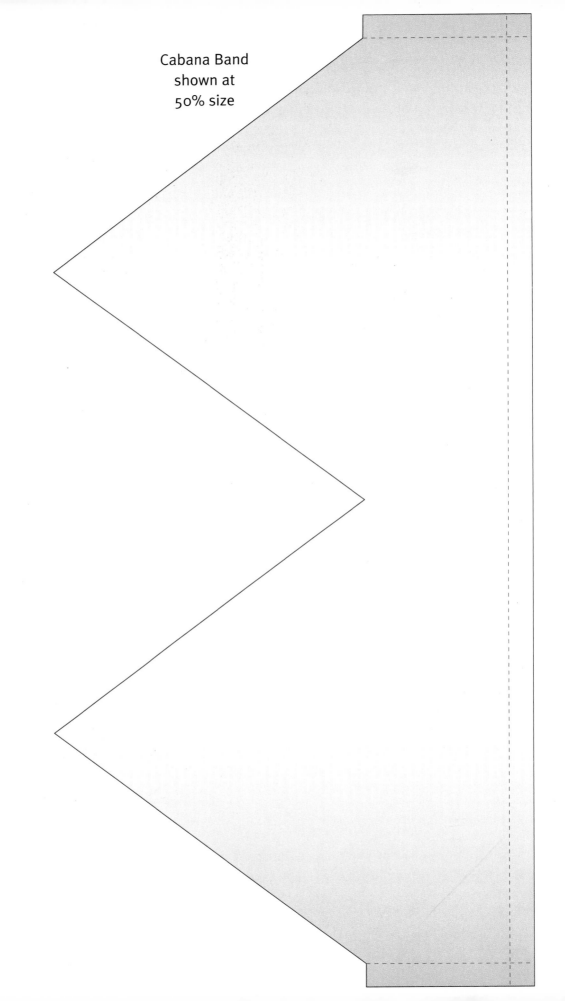

Cabana Band
shown at
50% size